CHAINED TREE, CHAINED OWLS

Also by
Catharine Savage Brosman

Poetry:

Watering (1972)
Abiding Winter (chapbook, 1983)
Journeying from Canyon de Chelly (1990)
Passages (1996)
The Swimmer and Other Poems (chapbook, 2000)
Places in Mind (2000)
Petroglyphs: Poems and Prose (chapbook, 2003)
The Muscled Truce (2003)
Range of Light (2007)
Breakwater (2009).
Trees in a Park (chapbook, 2010)
Under the Pergola (2011)
On the North Slope (2012)
On the Old Plaza (2014)
A Memory of Manaus (2017)

Non-fiction creative prose and short fiction:

The Shimmering Maya and Other Essays (1994)
Finding Higher Ground: A Life of Travels (2003)
Music from the Lake and Other Essays (2017)
An Aesthetic Education and Other Stories (2019)

(Continued on page 63)

Chained Tree, Chained Owls

Poems

Catharine Savage Brosman

Green Altar Books
Columbia, South Carolina

CHAINED TREE, CHAINED OWLS

Copyright ©2020 Catharine Savage Brosman

All rights reserved. No part of this publication may be reproduced, distributed, or transmitted in any form or by any means, including photocopying, recording, or other electronic or mechanical methods, without the prior written permission of the publisher, except in the case of brief quotations embodied in critical reviews and certain other noncommercial uses permitted by copyright law.

Published by Green Altar Books, an imprint of

Shotwell Publishing LLC

Post Office Box 2592

Columbia, South Carolina 29202

Original Cover Painting by Olivia McNeely Pass

Cover design by Boo Jackson Designs

FIRST EDITION

ISBN: 978-1-947660-32-8

Acknowledgments

Appreciation is due to the editors of the following periodicals for permission to reprint the poems indicated:

Abbeville Institute Newsletter: "At the Entrance to City Park," "Christ Church, Alexandria" (from "Monuments");

The Agonist (an Internet magazine): "In the Medicine Bow Range," "Front Range Rockies," "On the Flank of Pike's Peak," "Flag Mountain," "Gift of Cacti," "Caldera," "Wind-Turbine Field," "Notched Sky," "Guadalupe Mountains" (from "Landscapes");

Chronicles: A Magazine of American Culture: "Styles" (the series); "For One Lost at Sea in Wartime, Leyte Gulf" (from "Scenes"); "Prologue," "On Lee Circle, New Orleans," "Site of the Jefferson Davis Memorial, Canal Street," "Interlude: At the Supreme Court," "St. Louis," "Charlottesville," "Epilogue" (from "Monuments"); "St. David's, Wales," "The Cathedral Church of St. Martin, Leicester, England," "St. Andrews Cathedral, Scotland," "Notre-Dame de Chartres, France (Exterior)," "Notre-Dame de Chartres (Interior)," "St. Louis Cathedral, New Orleans," # 1 (from "Cathedrals");

Modern Age: "Aspen Grove," "Broken Landscape," "White Water" (from "Landscapes").

The author photograph, taken in the French Quarter of New Orleans, is by Joseph Warner.

This book is in memory of my parents and grandparents, my husband, Patric Savage (1928-2017), and my friend Evelyn Powell Payne (1935-2001).

It is likewise dedicated to my daughter, Kate Deimling, her husband, Brian, their children, Clara and Julian, my Colorado cousins, and my loyal and supportive friends, especially Patricia J. Teed

Contents

Introductory Note i
Preface by Way of Five Lines 1
Styles 3
Scenes 7
Roads Not Taken 13
Jean in the Snow Cave 17
Five in Memory of Patric 21
Monuments 25
Abroad 31
Towers 35
Cathedrals 39
Landscapes, I 43
Landscapes, II 47
Scènes, translated into French by Jeannine Hayat 51
Les Tours, translated into French by Jeannine Hayat .. 57
About the Author 61
About The Translator and Illustrator 62

Introductory Note

This collection of poems arose from a simple request to the author from D. C. Berry, a Mississippi poet, that she draft for him a few lines on the distinctions between Romanesque, or Norman, architecture and the Gothic style. Not that such information cannot be found in any suitable reference book, based on more authority, but following the principle that, in varied proportions, verse may have merits going beyond those of prose: precision, concision, incisiveness, and verbal beauty, which all lead to memorability. What Pope says of "true wit" applies well to poetry: "Nature to advantage dress'd." The first poem of "Styles" was the response to David Berry's request, which a prefatory poem here acknowledges. (The two poets have never met, but have corresponded in connection with his writing.) A few further requests, and additional poems, followed. Eventually, as the present author pursued the possibilities of the form, loose knots of themes and topics, like magnetized paper clips on a desk, drew in others, which made little clusters and then organized themselves into series. Soon the enterprise became a book, which can be dated May 2018–November 2019.

For the initial response, five lines seemed suitable as a form: short, but affording fifty syllables in iambic pentameter—a challenge, certainly, but more ample than a couplet or tercet. Somewhat like what Mallarmé called the sonnet, "un grand poème en petit," it allows for a few details and a bit of development, beyond the bare bones. A middle, as well as a beginning and an end, may emerge; it may show contrast or change, perhaps release of tension or a concluding spasm of pain. The rhyme scheme selected, *ababa*, provided the opportunity for variation, with contrasting echoes, combined with repetition (together, often the basis of music). For the present undertaking, the appeal of consistency as well as the general challenges and rewards of the form suggested that it should be maintained throughout. (Readers will note, however, one set of anapestic tetrameters and a few feminine rhymes.)

This five-line form is no invention. Edmund Waller used it, with an *ababb* scheme, in his "Go, Lovely Rose," and it is found among other poets of his period; but it is far less common than the quatrain. French poets, including two of the present writer's favorites, Charles Baudelaire and Guillaume Apollinaire, offer beautiful examples, among which are Baudelaire's "La Chevelure" and "Madrigal triste" and Apollinaire's long poem "La Chanson du mal aimé," a masterpiece of narrative and lyrical construction. In these examples, the stanza never stands alone, however, whereas in most cases here, five lines by themselves constitute an entire poem, discrete, without connection other than thematic and organizational to what follows.

The question then arose of what the stanza should be called. *Five-liner*, while an accurate and practical term, fits poorly into the standard vocabulary of prosody. The French term *quintil* does not seem to have entered English. According to the *Princeton Handbook of Poetic Terms*, the appealing *quintet*, which evokes another art also, applies only to a stanza of varying rhyme scheme as well as meter—a restriction that rules it out for the poems here. Why not *quintain*, a word that one sees occasionally? It has the merit of parallelism with the accepted *quatrain* and less familiar terms. And, without being a barbarism, given its etymology, it suggests a vein of novelty. Indeed, the author hopes that the poems will strike readers as fresh as well as pithy.

The fact, and the sense, of fate constitute a recurrent theme and dictate the mood of numerous quintains. Personal and historical destiny, and human responsibility for them, or free will (since "the fault lies not in our stars, but in ourselves"), appear

Introductory Note

side-by-side with what may be called natural destiny.[1] The cover painting, by Olivia McNeely Pass, highlights this presence by its reference to two quintains placed at the beginning of *Scenes*. The first evokes a massive hackberry tree on her property in Louisiana, around which some previous owner had wrapped a heavy chain; ailing, the tree had to be felled. The second evokes a bird show at a village fair on a Sunday afternoon in Evington, Leicestershire, upon which she, the present author, and their Leicester hostess, Margot Fawcett, happened. All three were appalled by the condition of the unfortunate creatures on display, suffering under such a malign fate.

The various parts of this collection are organized generally by topic, theme, mood, or setting. "Jean in the Snow Cave," an exception, has a narrative line. The two "Landscapes" sections, an exercise in seeing, follow a geographic and topographic line that begins in Wyoming and includes the Colorado-Wyoming border territory, then proceeds south through Colorado and New Mexico, ending in far Trans-Pecos Texas.

More than seventy poems, however brief, are too many to digest at one sitting, or even three or four. The author suggests either random browsing or proceeding by topic, theme, or setting, according to the reader's interest, with the table of contents as a guide. Footnotes clarify and amplify certain poems.

---

[1] The speaker is Cassius, in *Julius Caesar*, I, 2. Note that subsequently Caesar expresses a fatalistic view—that death, "a necessary end, will come when it will come" (II, 2).

Five Lines by Way of Preface

Dear David,
                You suggested one day that
I write for you short lines on modes and styles—
as *aide-mémoire*. One poem soon begat
a second, then a third (the Muse's wiles).
My snapshots are below.
                        Your friend The Cat

STYLES

1

The barrel vault, square pillars—solid, plain—
and rounded arches of the Romanesque
are stone *awake*. To Gothic style pertain
fine ribs, the pointed arch, and the grotesque,
with flying buttresses—a *dream*'s domain.

2

Irregular, ornate, the rococo,
encrusted, pastel-painted, crystal-lit,
abandons classic lines for dazzling show
of jeweled, textured, fluid, gilded wit—
self-proclamation, just a rooster's crow.

3

Rose window catching light from heaven's eyes,
the nave a-sail in majesty, and spires
upraised in prayer: what presence, what emprise!
—In kivas underground, dark sagebrush fires
burn low for nether gods, eyeless, yet wise.

4

It fell from outer space, I think—a swerve
from time, a whirlwind, called the Guggenheim,
affording old New York a modern verve,
though filled with cave art. Silly or sublime?
It's up to you. Go see. Don't lose your nerve!

Styles

5

Doric, Ionic, and Corinthian—
three orders left to us by genius Greeks—
hold up the temple sky, the mind of man,
harmonious. —Here's sunset, with great streaks
of mauve. Love beauty, mortals, while you can.

Scenes

Chained Tree: A Tribute

Surviving frost, erosion, hurricane,
the giant lasted long, asail on light—
though trimmed, or shackled, by a heavy chain
absorbed into its pith, a parasite.
—It's gone now, shorn and felled: the old refrain.

Chained Owls

Athena's birds perch, tethered fast by rope
or chain, forlorn, displayed against their will
for our amusement. By an avian hope
they try their wings, again, again, yet still
no flight, no grace—fate's pained, despairing trope.

Amputees' Ward

Sam Beckett put his *culs-de-jatte* in jars
or cans, discoursing on their ruined state.
You ride in wheelchairs or electric cars,
but trade old questions, old replies on fate;
and yet you speak of happy days and stars.[2]

Passage

Hans wanted me to help them each to die.
Imagine—my ineptitude, my dread!
They went abroad, "to visit friends." A lie?
Their nephew later wrote that both were dead.
—Two gracious angels, mercifully, stopped by.

---

[2] *Culs-de-jatte* is a French term for those whose lower limbs have been amputated or are paralyzed. The Samuel Beckett references are multiple, echoing *The Unnamable* (*L'Innommable*, 1953), *Happy Days*, 1961 *(Oh les beaux jours)*, *Play* (1964). The phrase "The same old questions, the same old answers, there's nothing like them" appears as such or with variations in a number of Beckett works, including *End-game (Fin de partie*, 1957). Note that Beckett's works usually appeared first in French, then English, but occasionally in the reverse order. The dates here are those of the earliest publication.

SCENES

BRIDAL TRAIN
—Paris, 2000

A marriage is a voyage, the seas unsure.—
"Au revoir!" The bride ran quickly, shed her train,
and dressed to take the TGV, a tour
in Italy. They'll dine on love, champagne.
What follows? Will they founder, or endure?

EX-WEDDING TRAIN
—Colorado, 1930

She came back on the westbound train, without
much comment, and alone. Where was her bliss—
that handsome husband, rich, in love, no doubt?
Thereafter she was always known as "Miss."
Some family facts are never talked about.

Summer Street Scene
—Colorado Springs

This town's a magnet—tourists, youth, the bum
who sleeps outdoors. A corner preacher brays,
foretelling how the Beasts of John will come;
an anarchist holds forth near two cafés.
The game of changing men is zero-sum.

Court Scene
—Colorado

We're on the tennis court, when two young deer
approach the fence. Eyes bright, they stop. *What's this?*
They stare: four bipeds running strangely, here,
then there; smack, streak, thud, smack, a lightning kiss,
a shout. Again! Is that how gods appear?

SCENES

For One Lost at Sea in Wartime, Leyte Gulf
—In memory of John Elliott Hill

No mournful cypress, gravel path, no stone
to mark your dying in these depths—all heave
and flow, the same in constant change, and lone;
no purchase by which memory might grieve,
just darkness underneath, the endless moan.

Oedipus in Great Age

Despite King Oedipus' immense ordeal,
his noble soul concluded all was well.
His sufferings were not beyond appeal;
they were an offering for the citadel,
and requisite reproof of the ideal.[3]

---

[3] In addition to suggesting the essence of a city—its identity, distinctiveness, strength—the word *citadel* here has an oblique connection to Antoine de Saint-Exupéry and his late book, *Citadelle*, in which he sets out his humanistic creed, by which he aspired to ideals of citizenship and cultivation of human potential, while acknowledging realistically the limits of human achievement.

Roads Not Taken

Royal Gorge Suspension Bridge

It's there, like Everest. So shall I drive
it, scrawny, just a thread? The Arkansas
below tears roughly down, as if alive.
I hesitate, then turn around. No raw
experience, thanks, few risks; I want to thrive.

The Wheel of Fortune

Fate favors irony, a twinkling star.—
The two men left the club, but stopped to chat.
One turned to go. His friend got in his car,
reversed, and felt a bump . . . . God, what was *that*?
The morgue's nearby; death did not travel far.

Mountain Train

We were to take a tourist train, but fire
has seared the mountains, melted trees and track,
and shut down Silverton. So which is wrier,
a scenic route that goes nowhere but back,
or riding to the dead ends of desire?

Journeys Ill-Taken
    — At the D. H. Lawrence Ranch, near Taos

He might have stayed, and lived— the surer tack.
Instead, he took the road to southern France—
old beauty, but Procrustes' bed, the rack.
He thought then of New Mexico, the dance
of death. His ashes made the journey back.

Stieglitz in New York

Why cross the Hudson? All he wished to do,
or photograph, was there, a mother lode,
while Georgia chose Ghost Ranch and Abiquiu,
a painter's land. He would not take that road—
that moonscape, light, the Pedernal askew.

Jean in the Snow Cave

—In memory of Jean A. H. Miller

1

No way to climb back down; the storm had caught
them out.   A strange mistake, since few could know
these mountains better.   Burrowing, they bought
a night's survival, bedded in the snow
and windless, free to brood in frozen thought.

2

By nature prudent, though dynamic, bold,
Jean had a hiker's winter gear—the bare
essentials. James had less. They ate, unrolled
thin sleeping bags, and wrapped themselves, aware
of little but the stark, embracing cold.

3

She heard him turning, seeking warmth, as though
it might materialize. She slept, till dream,
in which she spread a blanket on the snow
(her Hudson Bay), awakened her. The theme
would not release her mind— a maddening show.

4

She thought of Guillaumet, whose plane was wrecked
on Andes ice. He gave up on his life;
but, lower down, his body might reflect
the sun in snow melt and be found; his wife
would get insurance. Love has that effect.[4]

---

[4] The story of Henri Guillaumet was told by his fellow-aviator Saint-Exupéry in *Terre des hommes* (*Wind, Sand, and Stars*, 1939). Having crashed flying east from Santiago, Chile, and spent two nights by his wrecked plane, which he could not repair, he decided to attempt descending the rugged, frozen terrain. He was thinking, he reported, of his friends and especially his wife. "Si ma femme croit que je vis, elle croit que je marche." Without evidence of his death, she would have had to wait four years to collect his pilot's life insurance. Ignoring hunger and his desire to sleep—which could easily have meant dying too soon—he continued his painful descent until, a week later, he walked in. (Other flyers, including Saint-Ex, had looked for the wreckage, in vain.)

5

She slept again, and dreamt of alpenglow.
A brilliant world awaited them at dawn,
pink melon light on the arete, a floe
of crimson clouds. The storm was gone.
How commonplace the day would be, below!

Five in Memory of Patric

Book Collector

Pat fed on books, and when that appetite
declined (unopened catalogues, new buys
unread) he recognized how, finally, sight,
like mind, would change, the gift of altered eyes
accommodating him to glorious light.

Burial Deferred, # I

All Houston's watery from the hurricane
last week. And Pat lies uninterred; the flood
stopped all but death. To whom might I complain?
Can men dig graves in sodden grass and mud?
He waits, indifferent to love, to pain.

Burial Deferred, # 2

Pat was a witty man. He'd always take
his chance to make a pun, tell jokes, some clean,
sing Irish songs. He would have loved a wake—
impossible. At least the casket's green.
He's in a cooler now, preserved, opaque.

On the Liffey, Dublin

A year ago I mourned before his bier.
I stand now by the river of his heart,
the shore where he would wish to reappear.
But no. I grieve, and shall, yet live—apart;
he would not have survived me long, I fear.

Five in Memory of Patric

Among the Blest

I picture Pat up there, in starry halls,
a book in hand, with music of the spheres,
half-energy, half-mass, as he recalls
land's beauty, blue of ocean, tender tears—
or hitting cosmic dust for tennis balls.

Monuments

Prologue

The New People's Republic has launched its campaign,
much like Stalin and Hitler, like Mao, Pol Pot,
to remove all that's harmful, to launder my brain,
tear down statues, change language, impose tommyrot.
We must wipe out the past and repent. It's insane!

On Lee Circle, New Orleans

A foul *fait accompli*; an altered view.
As usual, fanatics are to blame,
and egos gratified by much ado.
But *Lee*, at least, will always be a name;
we cannot say the same of *you*, Landrieu.

At the Entrance to City Park

They couldn't stop with R. E. Lee, of course.
The cleansing must be thorough, the more to hurt
us. Beauregard is gone, thus; so's his horse.
But why just monuments—mere stone, inert?
We may be next—pure evil at its source.

Site of the Jefferson Davis Memorial, Canal Street

There's not much left; the pedestal and base,
the man himself, are gone, removed at night
by "Take Em Down," which didn't dare to face
the public. Yankees always had it right—
so like today's, who feast on our disgrace.

Interlude: At the Supreme Court

With law, life, marriage redefined, what's next?
Free drugs, polygamy, child sacrifice?
The country's overdosed and oversexed,
and crawls with illegality and lice.
Oh, Courts Supreme, unreason's metatext!

St. Louis

Two statues, undisturbed, stood in a park,
both honored officers, the South, the North.
The vandals pulled one down. That is a mark
of tyranny. Don't speak of peace, henceforth;
a winch still dangles somewhere in the dark.

Charlottesville

"It's all the fault of Mr. Jefferson,
who built his university for men,
all white. Now revolution has begun.
One statue's gone; it's time to move again.
Let's burn the library! Call out the Hun!"[5]

Christ Church, Alexandria

George Washington's own parish, where he prayed,
in thrall to fashion now, removes a plaque,
then two, to please the whiners. What his shade
may think I wonder. Quite the proper tack
for us is: show the stuff of which we're made.[6]

---

[5] The reference is not only to the swarming Huns who invaded Europe in the fourth and fifth centuries A.D. but also to twentieth-century Germans, who, following a comparison that Kaiser Wilhelm II himself introduced, were often called Huns, by the British and others, and not without reason. In 1914, for instance, in an act of greatly disproportionate retribution, the Germans set fire to and destroyed the library at Louvain (Leuven), Belgium, which contained medieval manuscripts, incunabula, and countless other priceless holdings.

[6] In October 2017 the authorities of Christ Church announced they would remove the plaque in honor of Washington, a parish supporter, and another honoring R. L. Lee.

Epilogue

This childish rage defies both circumstance
and sense. "Distractions"—so Confucius saith.
Look first to your own measures in the dance
of time, and leave alone men of good faith,
all patriots. Let Clio have a chance.[7]

---

[7] The mention of Clio underlines the importance of historical understanding.

Abroad

The Bloomsbury Hotel
—For J. W.

Quite fine, set back just off Great Russell Street,
it's new—an old girls' hostelry was razed.
So close to Tottenham Court Road, a seat
for social wrecks! Are filth and beauty phased,
sublunarly, by some osmotic feat?

Bloomsbury

In sybaritic ease, we drink and dine,
reflecting on the famed who "lived in squares"
but "loved in triangles." Their lives align
with tragedy—high station, fall. What prayers
could fit their fate, its terrible design?[8]

---

[8] The phrase, in its full form— "They lived in squares, painted in circles and loved in triangles"—is attributed to Dorothy Parker. The squares include Gordon Square, Russell Square, and Fitzroy Square. Personal drama marked the life of more than one writer and painter in the highly-talented and productive Bloomsbury Group, some of whom were bisexual or homosexual. These dramas include suicide; miserable love affairs, some triangular; jealousy; tense and broken marriages; and *ménages à trois*.

Wine-Tasting

The cream of Viennese society,
with Wachau Valley wines. Too bad that I'm
no oenophile. "This white —don't you agree?—
has overtones of apple, Grecian lime;
that Zweigelt red, of plum." Pure poetry!

Trieste

The main piazza spreads its classic grace
to seaward. Poor Carlotta took Trieste,
her husband's *Lustschloß*, as her ideal space
for happiness—the Habsburg Empire west.
She died insane, a remnant of her race.[9]

---

[9] Charlotte of Belgium (1840-1927), the last surviving child of Leopold I, married the brother of Franz-Joseph I, the archduke Maximilian (1832-1867), who, with the help of Napoleon III, became emperor of Mexico. It will be noted that she outlived her husband by sixty years. The castle, Miramare, on the outskirts of Trieste, was designed partly by him, but she also cherished it. She settled there upon returning from Mexico in 1866 with the purpose of seeking assistance for Maximilian from Napoleon III and the pope. From 1866 on, perhaps before, she suffered from paranoia and other mental and behavioral disorders; at times she was examined or treated by doctors. After Maximilian's execution and the fall of the Mexican empire, she did not remain long at Miramare; on orders, she returned to Belgium. She witnessed the fall of the Austro-Hungarian Empire at the end of World War I.

Abroad

Diocletian's Palace
—For the Deimlings

Crowds wander, on a scorching day in Split,
among the arches of the peristyle.
Two guards, with Roman breastplate, helmet, kit
of shield and dagger, pose for photos. —While
we're joined, we can't make past and present fit.

Volcano

Through Scylla and Charybdis, sailing's fine,
one's nerves unruffled. But Stromboli churns
its magma, belching, spewing out a line
of smoke and ash. Below, the forest burns,
telluric spirits discomposing mine.

Towers

Charles d'Orléans in the Tower of London

A hostage for a quarter-century
("a forest of long waiting"), valorous,
"The Mouse" endured, until at last set free
through former enemies' good will. To us,
his poems pay his ransom, handsomely.[10]

Montaigne's Tower

Retired from Bordeaux, he used his leisure
essaying what he was and knew—his tower
a happy refuge, apt for peace and pleasure:
to read, to write, to draw out wisdom's flower.
He rode four winds of thought, collecting treasure.

---

[10] Charles, duc d'Orléans (1394-1465) was taken prisoner on the field at Agincourt, where he was discovered fully armoured, alive but unable to rise from a mound of corpses. He was taken to England and kept at various castles, including the Tower of London, Fotheringhay, and Pontefract. An illuminated edition of his poems depicts his imprisonment in London. For dynastic reasons, Henry V of England forbade his release for ransom; only the death of key figures and changes in alliances make his return possible. One of his famous poems, in ballad form, "En regardant vers le pays de France," expresses his nostalgia for his homeland and hope of seeing it again.

Chateaubriand's Tower, Combourg

He kissed his father, reached his turret room,
the taunts still with him. He was not afraid,
however; they had made him hardy. Gloom
and specters followed him; but art repaid
him, well. What memories; what rare perfume![11]

Stendhal's Towers

He wrote of happy heights: a prison cell
(the tall Farnese Tower where Fabrice
discovered beauty), and the bosom swell
of fir-dressed mountains, offering release
and light to restless Julien Sorel.[12]

---

[11] Called "The Enchanter" for his exquisite prose style (perfumed, as it were), François-René de Chateaubriand (1768-1848) wrote about himself in *Mémoires d'outre-tombe*. Born in Saint-Malo, the tenth child of a Breton nobleman, the sensitive boy spent most of his youth in the eerie, haunted atmosphere of Combourg, an isolated château. In wintertime, his taciturn father paced the floor silently in the evenings, an almost spectral figure, dressed in a white robe and white bonnet. Nightly he taunted the boy by reminding him of resident ghosts.

[12] The Stendhal references are to *La Chartreuse de Parme* and *Le Rouge et le noir*. Fabrice was delighted by his lofty prison cell and the perspectives it offered over the Italian countryside; he also fell in love with the jailer's beautiful daughter. Julien, like his creator, hated everything somber, including the atmosphere and black-clad priests at the seminary where he was a student.

Towers

Vigny's Tower
— Maine-Giraud, France

Friends wondered at the force of his complaint.
Had he not won both love and fame? He pled,
with pride, his wounded genius, fate's constraint.
"Then Vigny to his ivory tower fled."
A hermitage does not make one a saint.[13]

Victor Hugo's Tower
— Hauteville House, Guernesey, the 1860s

He climbed his lookout tower, admiring the stain
of sunrise eastward. France! The emperor
still ruled, and Hugo swore he would remain
abroad. Who could imagine insults, war,
defeat, the wresting of Alsace-Lorraine?

---

[13] The phrase on the ivory tower is a condensation of lines by Charles-Augustin de Sainte-Beuve.

Cathedrals

St. David's, Wales

Of Norman style, it's strangely built *below*
the city. We descend. We're not alone;
the nave is full, and there's some sort of show,
with Brubeck's music on the saxophone—
as worship, quite a modern quid pro quo.

The Cathedral Church of St. Martin, Leicester, England

It was the parish church, then raised to seat
the bishop. A survivor—German bombs
nearby—it honors now a king's defeat,
on Bosworth Field, by those especial palms
for losers. Richard, death can yet be sweet.[14]

---

[14] The Church of St. Martin, dating from the eleventh century, served for a time as a bishop's seat, but the district lost the bishopric and for centuries thereafter belonged to one diocese after another. In 1926, a bishopric was reinstated, the church was renamed the next year. The city was in the flight path of German bombers heading to Coventry but was hit badly only in November 1940; the cathedral was spared. The remains of Richard III, called Crookback, were unearthed in 2012 under a car park not far from the cathedral. His deformed frame and DNA testing verified that the bones, the location of which was unknown for centuries, were his. He was reburied with great ceremony in 2015. An earlier cenotaph honoring him was replaced by a tomb of tasteful contemporary design, where white roses are often placed. His defeat led to the reign of the first Tudor king, Henry VII.

St. Andrews Cathedral, Scotland

The saint's remains are gone; much else. What's left—
an arch, an ancient tower, high broken wall—
holds cold remembrance. Still, by holy theft,
huge stones and beams, dispersed, survive, as stall,
fence, cottage, trough—the spirit's lowly heft.

Notre-Dame de Chartres (Exterior)

It's asymmetrical, a brief surprise,
admired, although, always, saints look odd—
stone-pocked, niched awkwardly, as if with eyes
apart from life, intent on only God.
That stern gaze is the vision of the wise.

Cathedrals

Notre-Dame de Chartres (Interior)

No light here save in color— saffron, red,
green, copper blue—from oxides in the beech
that fired the glass, and fires the soul. The dead
themselves, entombed, must feel the rays that reach
from heaven, and One who suffered in our stead.

Saint-Etienne de Metz

My cousin saw it, late in the campaign
with Bradley, driving east—a citadel
of yellow stone, for Christ and for Lorraine,
its colored glass half-gone to bomb and shell.
Chagall's blue windows glorify the stain.[15]

---

[15] The author's cousin-german, Elizabeth Bradshaw Michels, a generation older, was a surgical nurse in France with the U.S. Army, 1944-46.

The word *stain* may be taken in a theological sense (the stain of human error being redeemed by Christ's sacrifice and glory, alluded to often in Chagall's ecclesiastical art). It can point likewise, antiphrastically, to the cultural wrongs of the Germans, who, for example, deliberately shelled Rheims cathedral in World War I, and in the following war were responsible for destroying or damaging many churches, including the cathedral of Metz. The windows "half-gone to bomb and shell" dated from the nineteenth century. Stained glass of that period is considered inferior to medieval achievements and, in the present time, to Chagall's designs and the work of his craftsmen; hence the destruction of the old led to a glorious replacement. The name of the city is pronounced [mɛs].

St. Louis Cathedral, New Orleans
1

The jewel of Jackson Square, its form refined
for Gallic taste, presides at drunkenness,
crime, indolence—life's pleasures underlined—
an icon for man's nature, since excess
as well as lofty measure makes the mind.

2

The interface is really rather nice:
streets named for saints, but also Pirates' Alley;
cathedral, presbytère, corruption, vice,
three murders just this week, a common tally—
the more to magnify Christ's sacrifice.

Landscapes, I

Broken Landscape
— Wyoming

Around me, even slopes crack suddenly,
their green in ruptured ski runs; rocky breaks
appear, then heal. So did the plains agree
to rise, or mountains fall apart? It takes
a modern mind to read earth's history.

In the Medicine Bow Range

Land rises sharply here, when it's been freed
of urban burdens. Past Virginia Dale,
pale, misty vistas; clouds and earth, agreed,
wash off my restlessness. How green, how frail
is happiness. Its watercolors bleed.

Front Range Rockies

In creases, recesses, and knobs, they rise
to view, becoming outlines, hills, red rocks,
then peaks. Once there, among the folds, your eyes
lose range and sense; it's Escher's paradox,
outside turned in, a sleight-of-hand surprise.

On the Flank of Pike's Peak

This is the country of the Manitou,
with healing springs, great caves, and Fountain Creek,
"which boils." Beware, though, of such gods: they strew
their boulders by a shudder, lash the peak
with lightning, torch a canyon—flood it, too.

Landscapes, I

Flag Mountain

Precipitous, rough, much too steep for skiing,
thick-spread with spruce and aspen, pocked with stone,
this mountain lends itself, at least, to seeing,
both field and lookout point. Know and be known—
perspectives on the human mode of being.

Aspen Grove

The others hiked ahead; the grove's now mine,
its lighting tinseled, cool. The forest floor
is blue with lupine, harebell, columbine.
Green music runs, abstracted; cirrus score
the sky. Do I imagine the design?

Landscapes, II

White Water
                —Along the Arkansas River

Rough canyon, rougher waters, forced apart
by shoals and fallen boulders, in a field
of moiling, eddying—the maelstrom heart
of doubt— until, downstream, commotions yield
to pools, serene, the apogee of art.

Caldera
                —New Mexico

The center's green, the edges dark, volcanic,
where lava spewed, flowed, cooled to primal turds,
ur-fire and brimstone, tools of the satanic,
yet less than minds—cloacae—that turn words,
a prize, to mischief, murderous, tyrannic.

Gift of Cacti

A landscape crowded in an earthen bowl
composing beauty— stones, a crimson bloom,
and seven succulents, a mini-scroll
of desert life. Oh, Ellen! And there's room
for friendship, thirsty, patient—soil and soul.

Wind-Turbine Field

They twirl their blades in measured ecstasy,
corralling rebel currents. I am caught,
like them, in circumstance, the spirit free
but channeled. What an airy field of thought!
I whirl, to seize the day, impossibly.

Landscapes, II

Notched Sky
—In the Sangre de Cristo Range

The sky's indented sharply here, at pains
to show distinction, or to take a bite
of earth. Imagine! . . . bread for gods, the grains
informed as boulders, and transfigured light
at dawn, the wine of Christ in glorious stains.

Guadalupe Mountains

Time buried a lagoon, filled in its reef—
their passage marked in caves and canyons, zones
of meaning, fossilized. Leave disbelief;
imagine watery beings, algae, bones
turned immemorial. Time thought it brief.

Scènes, translated into French by Jeannine Hayat

À un arbre enchaîné: hommage

Rescapé du gel, de l'érosion, de l'ouragan,
le géant a prospéré, cinglant vers la lumière—
orné ou entravé par une lourde chaîne
incrustée dans sa moelle comme un parasite.
—Il n'est plus, étêté puis abattu, l'éternelle rengaine.

Chouettes enchaînées

Les oiseaux d'Athéna se perchent, attachés ferme à une corde
ou à une chaîne, désolés, exhibés malgré eux
pour notre divertissement. Poussés par leur espoir d'oiseau
ils battent des ailes encore et encore, pourtant
ni vol, ni grâce—image d'un destin pénible et désespéré.

Passage

Hans voulait que je les aide à mourir.
Imaginez mon désarroi, mon effroi!
Ils sont partis à l'étranger, chez des amis. Un mensonge?
Plus tard leur neveu m'a annoncé leur mort.
Par bonheur, deux anges gracieux se sont arrêtés.

Salle des amputés

Sam Beckett a installé ses culs-de-jatte dans des jarres
ou des bidons; ils dissertent sur leur vie ruinée.
Qu'on conduise un fauteuil roulant ou sa voiture,
on recycle les vieilles questions et les vieilles réponses sur le destin:
mais on parle des jours heureux et des étoiles.

Le train nuptial
         —Paris, 2000

Le mariage est une traversée, la mer incertaine.
"Au revoir !" À la hâte, la mariée s'est débarrassée de sa traîne,
habillée pour le TGV et le voyage
en Italie. Ils dîneront au champagne en amoureux.
Et ensuite ? Vont-ils couler ou endurer ?

Le train de l'ex-mariage
         —Colorado, 1930

Elle est rentrée à bord d'un train pour l'ouest, sans
beaucoup de commentaires et seule. Où était son bonheur ?
le beau mari, riche et sans doute amoureux ?
Par la suite elle fut connue comme une « Mademoiselle ».
Motus sur certains événements familiaux.

Scène estivale de rue
                              —Colorado Springs

Cette ville est un aimant—des touristes, des jeunes, des clochards
qui dorment dehors. Dans un coin un prédicateur mugit:
il annonce l'arrivée des bêtes de Jean;
un anarchiste pérore devant deux cafés.
Le jeu pour changer les hommes a pour somme zéro.

Scène sur un court de tennis
                                    —Colorado

Nous sommes sur un court de tennis, quand deux jeunes cerfs
approchent de la clôture. Les yeux brillants, ils s'arrêtent.
    Qu'est-ce que c'est?
Ils observent quatre bipèdes qui courent étrangement, d'abord ici,
puis là, un coup, un éclair, un bruit sourd, un coup, un baiser vif,
un cri. Encore une fois! Est-ce ainsi que le créateur se montre?

À UN MORT DISPARU EN MER PAR TEMPS DE GUERRE
—Golfe de Leyte

Pas un cyprès mélancolique, aucun sentier de gravier,
   pas de stelle
pour signaler la mort en ces profondeurs; tout est flux
et reflux, identique, sans cesse mouvant et isolé;
aucune expropriation dont la mémoire pourrait souffrir,
juste l'obscurité des profondeurs, la plainte sans fin.

ŒDIPE EN SON GRAND ÂGE

Malgré le supplice intense du roi Œdipe
sa noble âme a conclu à l'acceptation.
Ses souffrances ne manquaient pas d'intérêt;
elles valaient comme offrande à la citadelle,
et comme utile objection à l'idéal.

Les Tours, translated into French by Jeannine Hayat

Charles d'Orléans dans la Tour de Londres

Otage pour un quart de siècle dans
« la forêt de longue attente », valeureux,
« la souris » a tout enduré avant d'être enfin libéré,
par la grâce de ses anciens ennemis.   Pour nous,
ses poèmes paient sa rançon, généreusement.

La tour de Montaigne

Éloigné de Bordeaux, il s'*essayait* durant ses loisirs
à exprimer ce qu'il était et savait—sa tour était
un refuge heureux, bon à la paix et au plaisir
de lire, d'écrire et de découvrir la fleur de la sagesse.
Il suivait quatre pensées à la fois, amassant des trésors.

La tour de Chateaubriand, Combourg

Il embrassait son père, gagnait sa cellule dans la tour,
ses sarcasmes en tête. Il n'avait pas peur
pourtant: on l'avait endurci. Les ténèbres
et les spectres le poursuivaient, mais l'art le comblait;
quels souvenirs, quel parfum rare!

Les tours de Stendhal

Il décrivait des sommets heureux: une cellule de prison
(la haute tour de Farnèse où Fabrice
avait appris la beauté), et les formes bombées
de la montagne revêtue de pins, offrant liberté et lumière
à l'impatient Julien Sorel.

La tour de Vigny
                —Maine-Giraud, France

Ses amis s'étonnaient qu'il se plaigne si fort.
N'avait-il pas gagné amour et célébrité ? Avec orgueil
il invoquait son génie blessé, un destin borné.
« Et Vigny comme en sa tour d'ivoire rentrait ».
L'ermitage ne fait pas le saint.

La tour de Victor Hugo
                —Hauteville House, Île de Guernesey

Il montait à sa tour de vigie, admirait vers l'Est les teintes
du lever de soleil. France ! L'empereur
gouvernait toujours et Hugo jurait rester
à l'étranger. Qui pour imaginer les insultes, la guerre,
la défaite, la cession de l'Alsace-Lorraine ?

About the Author

Catharine Savage Brosman is Professor Emerita of French at Tulane University and Honorary Research Professor at the University of Sheffield. She has published eleven collections of poetry, of which the latest is *A Memory of Manaus* (2017). Her third volume of familiar essays, *Music from the Lake*, came out in 2017. During more than five decades, her verse appeared frequently all over America, especially in the *Sewanee Review* and *Southern Review*. She is the author or editor of numerous studies in French literary history, notably *Fiction, Art, Ideology: Images of War in France* (1999), as well as studies in American literature: *Louisiana Creole Literature* (2013) and *Southwestern Women Writers and the Vision of Goodness* (2016). *Louisiana Poets: A Literary Guide*, for which her co-author is Olivia McNeely Pass, appeared in 2019. A companion volume by Brosman on Mississippi poets will be released in summer 2020. In 2019 Green Altar Books, an imprint of Shotwell Publishing, issued her collected short fiction, *An Aesthetic Education and Other Stories*. For years, she and her late husband, Patric, spent their summers in Colorado, where she was born.

About the Translator

Jeannine Hayat, *agrégée d'université*, teaches French literature at the Lycée Racine in Paris. Her publications include *Jules Roy: Ombre et présence d'Albert Camus* and translations of fiction by the nineteenth-century American writer Constance Fenimore Woolson. In addition, she has translated poetry and prose by Nelson Algren, Barry Gifford, Paul Ruffin, and Catharine Savage Brosman. Translations of the latter's poems have appeared in *La Nouvelle Revue Française*, *Europe: Revue littéraire mensuelle*, and *Le Cerf-Volant*.

About the Illustrator

Olivia McNeely Pass, a Louisiana native who lives in St. Francisville, Louisiana, is retired from the English faculty of Nicholls State University but continues to teach from time to time at schools in the Baton Rouge area. Her paintings have won numerous prizes. She is co-author of *Louisiana Poets: A Literary Guide*.

Also by
Catharine Savage Brosman
(continued)

Scholarly books:
André Gide: l'évolution de sa pensée religieuse (1962)

Malraux, Sartre, and Aragon as Political Novelists (1964)

Roger Martin du Gard (1968)

Jean-Paul Sartre (1983)

Jules Roy (1988)

French Novelists, 1900-1930 (Dictionary of Literary Biography, 65), ed. with a foreword (1988)

French Novelists, 1930-1960 (Dictionary of Literary Biography, 72), ed. with a foreword (1988)

French Novelists since 1960 (Dictionary of Literary Biography, 83), ed. with a foreword (1989)

Art as Testimony: The Work of Jules Roy (1989)

An Annotated Bibliography of Criticism on André Gide, 1973-1988 (1990)

Simone de Beauvoir Revisited (1991)

Nineteenth-Century French Fiction Writers, 1800-1860: Romantics and Realists (Dictionary of Literary Biography, 119), ed. with an introduction (1992)

Nineteenth-Century French Fiction Writers, 1860-1900: Naturalists and Beyond (Dictionary of Literary Biography), ed. with an introduction (1992)

Twentieth-Century French Culture, 1900-1975, ed. with an introduction (Detroit: Gale, 1995)

Retour aux "Nourritures terrestres": Le Centenaire d'un bréviaire, ed. David H. Walker and Catharine Savage Brosman (1997)

Visions of War in France: Fiction, Art, Ideology (1999)

Existential Fiction (Detroit: Gale, 2000)
Albert Camus (Detroit: Gale, 2000)
Louisiana Creole Literature: A Historical Study (2013)
Southwestern Women Writers and the Vision of Goodness (2016)
Louisiana Poets: a Literary Guide, with Olivia McNeely Pass (2019)

SOUTHERN LITERATURE is the glory of American culture. Faulkner, O'Connor, Warren, Lytle, Davidson, Gordon, Percy, Chappell, Berry will be known as long as Western civilization survives and long after today's politicians, "experts," and celebrity writers are forgotten. Another of the greats, George Garrett, wrote that "all signs indicate that Southern literature, far from being on its last legs and far from representing a falling off from earlier and better days, seems very much alive." Shotwell Publishing supports Garrett's witness by launching the imprint Green Altar Books—a collection of Southern Literature.

www.ingramcontent.com/pod-product-compliance
Lightning Source LLC
LaVergne TN
LVHW020938090426
835512LV00020B/3412